Aunt Clara Brown

Official Pioneer

by Linda Lowery

illustrations by Janice Lee Porter

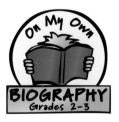

Carolrhoda Books, Inc./Minneapolis

The photograph on page 47 appears courtesy of the Colorado Historical Society.

This book is available in two editions:
Library binding by Carolrhoda Books, Inc.
Soft cover by First Avenue Editions
A Division of the Lerner Publishing Group
241 First Avenue North, Minneapolis, MN 55401 U.S.A.

Website address: www.lernerbooks.com

Library of Congress Cataloging-in-Publication Data

Lowery, Linda.
    Aunt Clara Brown: official pioneer / by Linda Lowery ; illustrations by Janice Lee Porter.
       p.   cm.
    Summary: A biography of the freed slave who made her fortune in Colorado and used her money to bring other former slaves there to begin new lives.
    ISBN: 1-57505-045-5 (lib. bdg.)
    ISBN: 1-57505-416-7 (pbk.)
    1. Brown, Clara, 1800-1885—Juvenile literature. 2. Afro-American women pioneers—Colorado—Biography—Juvenile literature. 3. Women pioneers—Colorado—Biography—Juvenile literature. 4. Free Afro-Americans—Colorado—Biography—Juvenile literature. 5. Frontier and pioneer life—Colorado—Juvenile literature. 6. Central City (Colo.)—Biography—Juvenile literature. [1. Brown, Clara, 1800-1885. 2. Afro-Americans—Biography. 3. Women—Biography. 4. Frontier and pioneer life—Colorado. 5. Colorado—History—To 1876.] I. Porter, Janice Lee, ill. II. Title.
F785.N4L69   1999
978.8'00496073'0092—dc21
[B]   98-24259

Manufactured in the United States of America
1 2 3 4 5 6 - SP - 04 03 02 01 00 99

To Kay Negesh, who keeps Clara's adventurous life alive through storytelling, and who inspired me to write this book—L.L.

For Wendy and Ana—J.P.

Clara Brown made her way past
barrels of dried fish.
She stepped around bales of cotton.
Everywhere, men tossed bags and boxes
from boats onto the dock.

They had brought all their belongings
down the Mississippi River to St. Louis.
Soon they would load up their
covered wagons and head west.
Stories about gold in the
Rocky Mountains ran wild.
Everybody hoped to get rich.

Clara walked up to a group of strangers.
She asked if they were going to Colorado.
A big, burly man turned.
What was a woman doing on the dock?
And a black woman at that?
He looked her up.
He looked her down.
Then he told Clara she couldn't
leave Missouri.
She was a slave.
Clara proudly waved the papers
in her hand.
Raising up her chin, she said
she was no slave.
She was Clara Brown, and these
were her freedom papers.

The men stared at Clara.

In 1859, not many slaves had been freed.

But when Clara's last owner had died,

Clara bought her own freedom.

It had taken a lot of money

and a lot of work.

But 57-year-old Clara was a free woman.

Clara told the men she couldn't

pay her way to Colorado.

But she would work for them.

These men looked like they were too busy

thinking about getting rich

to fix food or wash clothes.

Clara said she would cook their meals

and wash their shirts.

Smiles brightened the men's faces.

The man in charge of the group
stepped toward Clara.
"My name is Colonel Wadsworth,"
he said.
Right then and there, Clara Brown knew
she was heading west.

Clara hurried home to pack up her
laundry tub and boiler.
Her best friend, Becky Johnson, helped.
Becky was excited for Clara.
The gold miners were getting rich
out west.
Would Clara get rich, too?

Tears suddenly stung Clara's eyes.
It would be nice to be rich.
But she was really going to Colorado
for another reason.
She hoped her daughter Eliza Jane
would be there.
Clara wanted to see her sweet face
just one more time.

Clara had been sold many times
to many different slave owners.
She had lived in Virginia, Kentucky,
Kansas, and Missouri.
Twenty-five years earlier, the Kentucky
owner had sold Eliza Jane.
She was only 10.
Clara had never seen her again.
The minute Clara was free in 1856,
she had begun looking for Eliza.
She asked everyone she met
if they had seen her.
She watched the faces of people
passing by, hoping to spot her.
That's why Clara was heading west.
She thought Eliza's owners might have
taken her there.

The next morning, with loud shouts and
ox snorts, the wagon train pulled out.
Every wagon was piled high.
There were heavy tools for mining.
There were bags of flour and rice,
bushels of apples, boxes of tea.

Most of the men came alone.

A few brought their wives.

Clara took care of everybody.

Every day, she cooked the meals
over the campfire.

She hung buffalo meat to dry into jerky.

When people got sick, Clara nursed them
with teas and herbs.

Still, the men did not know how
to treat Clara.

She was not allowed to ride in the wagons.
Every day, she walked beside the oxen.
At night, the men argued about whether
slaves should be free.
They argued about where
Clara should sleep.
Should she sleep in the wagons
with the other women?
Or should she sleep
outside with the cattle?
The men did not know Clara's mother
had been a Cherokee Indian.
Had they known, it would have been
worse for Clara.
Clara ended up sleeping on the ground,
under a wagon.
She walked 680 miles.

In June of 1859, the wagon train made it
to Denver, Colorado.
Clara was tired, but thrilled.
Here in Colorado, she would start
a new life for herself.

Central City, Colorado
1859

Denver was buzzing with rumors
about gold.
People said Central City was the heart
of gold country.
But Denver was a long way
from Central City.
It was a two-week trip, 40 miles up
dangerous mountain roads.
The only way to get there was by coach.
However, black people were not allowed
on public coaches.

Clara had enough money to pay a man
to drive her in a private coach.
But she had to pretend she was
the driver's servant.
No one could know she had
paid him for the ride.
She was breaking the law.
She could go to jail.
Luckily, Clara and her laundry tub
arrived safely.

The St. Louis dock had been
crowded and noisy.
But it was sleepy compared to
Central City, Colorado.
Miners carried guns.
Fist fights broke out on street corners.

It was hard to sleep at night with all the
screaming and shooting.
People seemed to be just a little crazy
from striking gold.
Still, Clara was so happy to be there
that she set up shop within a few days.

Clara's laundry was the first in Colorado.

After all her years working as a slave,

Clara had become an excellent laundress.

Gold miners flocked to her laundry.

Soon she was making 50¢ a shirt.

This was a lot of money at that time.

In 1859, 50¢ would buy five

loaves of bread.

Clara quickly learned how to get her

money to make more money for her.

She bought land in Denver, Boulder, and
Idaho Springs, Colorado.
She bought seven houses in Central City.
Within a few years, she had $10,000
in land and money.
Clara Brown was rich.
Still, every day she waited for news
of Eliza Jane.

No one in Central City had news.

Clara's friend Becky had no news.

All the money in the world could not

bring Clara what she most wanted—to see

her daughter again.

While Clara was living in Colorado,

the Civil War began.

People in the Southern states did not want

slaves to be free.

People in the Northern states wanted

slavery to end.

Soldiers fought for four years.

In 1865, the war ended.

Soon after, all slaves were freed.

Clara decided to look for her daughter

one more time.

She would go to Kentucky.
That's where Eliza Jane had been
born into slavery.
That's where Clara hoped her daughter
would be.

Kentucky
1866

Clara shut down her laundry and made

the long trip back to Kentucky.

Everything was different

when she arrived.

The Civil War had left homes and

families ruined.

Many huge plantations were gone.

People who had been slaves had no idea

where to find work.

They had no homes and no money.

Some of them were living in camps,

wondering what to do.

Clara met many freed slaves.

She asked them all if they knew a woman

named Eliza Jane.

She traveled from town to town.

She went from camp to camp.

No one seemed to know her daughter.

Clara felt lonely and lost.

Her heart broke over and over again

when there was no news of Eliza.

All through her life, Clara had believed

that God helped her in hard times.

So she asked God to show her

what to do.

Her prayers told her to start

a whole new family.

It would be a family of people like

Clara and Eliza.

They would be people who could not find

their parents or their children.

Clara counted her money.

She had enough to bring 26 newly freed
slaves back to Colorado with her.

Some were relatives.

Most were strangers.

With Clara in charge, her new "family"
headed west on a wagon train.
This time, everyone's fare was paid
and they rode in the wagons.
Nobody walked.
In 1860, there had been only 23
black people in all of Denver.
Just six years later, Clara
came home with her "family" of 26.

The freed slaves made big news.
The newspapers said they arrived in
Colorado singing and dancing.
Clara gave each person a home
or a piece of land.
She taught them how to start their
own businesses.
In return, they spread the word
about Eliza Jane.

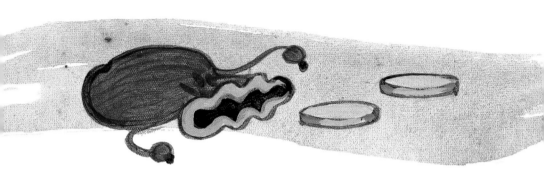

Within a few years, Clara's fortune
was gone.
She was cheated out of some of it
by unjust business people.
She lost some of her land in a flood.
Still, she felt rich.
Her money had paid for many people
to start new, free lives.
But Clara was growing old.
She needed money to take care of herself.
When pioneers got old, the state of
Colorado paid them in return for all the
work they had done settling the land.
The money was called a pension.

Anyone who settled in Colorado
before 1865 was an official pioneer.
Clara had arrived in 1859.
But when she tried to get her pension,
she discovered some strange rules.

All official pioneers had to be white.

And all official pioneers had to be men.

A black woman could not receive

a pioneer pension.

Clara had become famous for

her kindness.

She had always helped people who were

hungry or sick or treated badly because of

the color of their skin.

Everyone called her "Aunt" Clara Brown.

This time, it was her turn to ask for help.

Clara talked to her friends.

They thought she had done as much for

Colorado as any miner or rancher

had done.

They wrote letters to the newspapers.

They gave speeches at city hall about

Clara's problem.

The rules were changed.
Aunt Clara Brown became the
first official Colorado pioneer
who was not a white man.
She received the pension she deserved.

Council Bluffs, Iowa
1883

When Clara was in her 80s, she got a
letter from her old friend Becky Johnson.
Becky had moved to Iowa.
Clara was growing blind.
She squinted to read Becky's news.

Becky had met a woman at the post office
whose name was Eliza Jane.

She had been a slave.

She was taken from her mother
when she was 10 or 11.

Clara's heart just about stopped.

Could it be her daughter?

"Come right away," the letter read.

But Clara did not have enough
money to go.
Clara's friends heard the news.
They wrote newspaper articles and held
dinners to get money for her trip.
Finally, in early spring, Clara got on a train
bound for Council Bluffs, Iowa.

On the way, her mind wandered back to
Kentucky, 50 years before.

She remembered her little girl in her pink
dress, standing up on the stage for sale.

Eliza Jane was so scared that she threw up
in front of the crowd.

This made her owner angry.

He'd get less money for her if she
looked sickly.

Clara had wanted to push away all those
white people and rush up on the stage.
She wanted to take her little girl back
and hold her tight to her heart.
Instead, Eliza Jane was sold.
She was loaded on a wagon with farm
equipment, furniture, and other slaves.
Clara and Eliza didn't even get a chance
for a last hug.

Clara's train arrived in Council Bluffs.
There, she got on a trolley to
Second Street.
The closer Clara got to her stop,
the faster her heart beat.
All the passengers could see that
Clara was nervous.
They made sure she got off
at the right place.

Clara stepped off the trolley into
the brisk March wind.
She squinted into the sleet.

She saw a tall, dark woman running
toward her through the puddles.
Suddenly, Clara was struck with fear.
What if she did not recognize
her daughter?
It had been so many, many years.
The woman slowed down and came
closer.
Clara could just make out
her nose and her smile.

The woman took another shy step
forward.
Then Clara was close enough
to see her eyes.
They were the sweet brown eyes Clara
had never, ever forgotten.
Her heart leapt.
She would recognize her little girl
anyplace, even if a hundred years
had gone by.

Clara opened her arms.

Eliza Jane fell into her embrace.

Clara felt like the richest woman
in the world.

She was holding her own Eliza Jane
in her arms again.

And this time, she would never let her go.